LET'S TALK

Resting ▶ Forgiving ▶ Being Free ▶ and More

LET'S TALK

Resting ▶ Forgiving ▶ Being Free ▶ and More

Ken Ogorek

Steubenville, Ohio
A Division of Catholics United for the Faith
www.emmausroad.org

Emmaus Road Publishing
827 North Fourth Street
Steubenville, OH 43952

© 2011 by Ken Ogorek
All rights reserved. Published 2010
Printed in the United States of America
<15 14 13 12 11   1 2 3 4>

Library of Congress Control Number: 2010928686
ISBN: 978-1-931018-63-0

Scripture quotations are from Revised Standard Version of the Bible—
Second Catholic Edition (Ignatius Edition)
Copyright © 2006 National Council of the
Churches of Christ in the United States of America.
Used by permission. All rights reserved.

Unless otherwise indicated, Scripture quotations are taken from the Revised
Standard Version, Catholic Edition (RSVCE) © 1965, 1966 by the Division of
Christian Education of the National Council of the Churches of Christ in the
United States of America. Used by permission.

Excerpts from the English translation of the
Catechism of the Catholic Church for use in the
United States of America copyright © 1994,
United States Catholic Conference, Inc.—Libreria Editrice Vaticana.
Used with Permission. Noted as "CCC" in the text.

Cover design and layout by
Theresa Westling

Cover and inside artwork drawn by:
Natalie Rees, a senior at
Madonna High School, Weirton, WV.

Nihil Obstat: Rev. Daniel J. Mahan, STB, STL, *Censor Librorum*
Imprimatur: ✠ Most Reverend Daniel M. Buechlein, OSB, Archbishop of Indianapolis
November 16, 2009

The *Nihil Obstat* and *Imprimatur* are official declarations
that a book or pamphlet is free of doctrinal or moral error.
No implication is contained therein that those who have
granted the *Nihil Obstat* and *Imprimatur* agree with
the contents, opinions, or statements expressed.

To my children, to the youth of today, and to all who remain young at heart—continuing to grow in wisdom, age, and grace. (Luke 2:52)

Table of Contents

Note to the Youth Minister ix

Jump In x

Introduction xi

Discussion 1: Let's Talk about...
Thirst and the Eucharist 1

Discussion 2: Let's Talk about...
Where You Live and the Sacrament of Penance 7

Discussion 3: Let's Talk about...
Getting some Rest and the Anointing of the Sick 15

Discussion 4: Let's Talk about...
Your Plans and the Sacrament of Holy Orders 21

Discussion 5: Let's Talk about...
Your Strengths and the Sacrament of Marriage 27

Discussion 6: Let's Talk about...
Your Decisions and Freedom 35

Discussion 7: Let's Talk about...
Tobacco and the Fifth Commandment 43

Discussion 8: Let's Talk about...
Drugs and Sex 51

Responses to the Discussion Questions 59

Abbreviations

Second Vatican Council
GS *Gaudium et Spes*
(Pastoral Constitution on the Church in the Modern World, December 7, 1965)

NOTE TO THE YOUTH MINISTER

Each installment of *Let's Talk* contains material to initiate and facilitate discussion. The "Deeper Conversation" section provides references to Scripture and to points in the *Compendium of the Catechism of the Catholic Church*, offering follow-up information for each discussion. Responses to the "Discussion Time" questions can be found at the end of the book.

In addition, a "Youth Minister's Guide" is available at the website of Emmaus Road Publishing (emmausroad.org). Here you will find helpful tips on how to effectively use *Let's Talk* in a youth ministry setting.

JUMP IN

What would you rather do—listen to a lecture or have a discussion? Most teens (and most adults for that matter) will say they'd rather have a discussion.

While a great lecture can be enlightening, discussions are usually more enjoyable. For a discussion to be truly beneficial, though, it helps if it's based on some background information; otherwise it's just a bunch of people giving opinions with no helpful education happening.

Let's Talk is exactly what it says—a chance for you to have some great discussions. Background information is provided so that your discussion actually goes somewhere. *Let's Talk* covers a variety of topics and, over time, allows you to discuss every basic aspect of life and faith.

Why? You have rights. Some of your basic rights include life, education, and respect.

Every person has a right to hear our Catholic faith proclaimed in its entirety, at an age-appropriate level (which means several times in a lifetime). But "proclaiming the Faith" doesn't have to mean boring. *Let's Talk* allows you to interact with your heritage—the Catholic faith—without leaving any gaps and without a bunch of needless repetition.

So what do you say? Do you like discussions? Are you open to learning more about your Catholic faith? Let's talk.

INTRODUCTION

If you're like most teenagers, you probably get up around 5:00 a.m., bright-eyed and ready to face that brand-new day. Just kidding.

Sleeping in (or otherwise getting rest), using newfound freedom to make good choices, learning not to hold grudges—these are all life experiences that prepare us to know God better, and by this knowledge find out who we really are.

Are you ready to find out more about yourself, your friends, and your future? Let's talk.

Let's Talk About...
Thirst and the Eucharist

Discussion 1

"I'm thirsty." You've thought it. You've probably said it. People try to quench their thirst many different ways. And there are many different kinds of thirst. Our souls thirst for the Lord, who provides for us in the Eucharist our spiritual food, the Bread of Life, and our spiritual drink.

LET'S LISTEN

- The Church's life has a summit and a heart: it is the Eucharist. (See CCC 1407.*)
- A Eucharistic liturgy, or Mass, always includes
    - proclaiming the Word of God;
    - thanking our heavenly Father;
    - consecrating the bread and wine; and,
    - receiving the Body and Blood of Christ. (See CCC 1408.)
- The past touches our present when we celebrate the Eucharist. In the Eucharist the saving action of Jesus becomes present. (See CCC 1409.)

---

* The *Catechism of the Catholic Church* (CCC) is available at www.vatican.va/archive/ccc/index.htm

- Jesus offered His life only once and for all of us; yet through the work of our priest at Mass, this sacrifice is made present so that we can witness it, participate in it, and live it. (See CCC 1410.)
- Men who are legitimately ordained priests are the only ones who can preside at the Eucharist. (See CCC 1411.)
- What are the Eucharist's essential signs?
  - wheat bread
  - grape wine (see CCC 1412)
- The Holy Spirit's blessing is called down upon these elements, and the priest consecrates them: "This is my body which will be given up for you. . . . This is the cup of my blood."

LET'S REFLECT

To receive Jesus in Holy Communion you must be in a state of grace. If you are aware of mortal sin in your life, our loving Father has revealed that celebrating the Sacrament of Penance is required before you receive Communion. (See CCC 1415.) Because you increase your loving union with Jesus by receiving Him in the Blessed Sacrament, receiving this sacrament also strengthens the unity of His Mystical Body—our Church. (See CCC 1417.)

THIRST AND THE EUCHARIST

> *"The Church makes a big deal about the Eucharist. Some Christians worship in places where the Eucharist is barely even mentioned. When I understand what the Eucharist is, or really Who I receive in this sacrament—Jesus—then the focus of my Catholic faith on the Eucharist makes perfect sense. Why wouldn't we emphasize this most holy sacrament?"*

 **LET'S TALK!**

1. What is your reaction to the truth that time and space are temporarily suspended at Mass—that the past and Jerusalem really touch our present time and place?

2. Participating in Mass is worshipping God as He prefers. What does this say about:
   - considering attendance at another worship service instead of Mass on a Sunday or Holy Day of Obligation?
   - missing Mass without having a very serious reason for doing so?

3. Why do you think our Church asks us to be free of mortal sin if we intend to receive Jesus in Holy Communion?

4. What is the relationship between union with Jesus and unity in our Church?
   - Based on what you've learned about the Mass, if you and some friends were to attend Mass together once a week for a

month or two (outside of your usual weekly Sunday Mass), what does each of you think some of the benefits would be?

 ## ON A RELATED NOTE

Your Church takes liturgy so seriously that several of her most basic guidelines (precepts) relate to it. The precepts of the Church are

➤ Attend Mass on Sundays and holy days of obligation.
➤ Confess your sins at least once a year.
➤ Receive your Creator in Holy Communion at least during the Easter season.
➤ In addition to liturgy on Holy Days, you should keep them truly holy as you would a Sunday.
➤ Observe prescribed days of abstinence and fasting.
➤ According to your abilities provide for our Church's material needs. (See CCC 2042, 2043.)

 ## DRIVING IT HOME

Ask your parents what they were taught happens when the Holy Spirit is called down upon the bread and wine and your priest pronounces the words of consecration. (This is a good chance to make sure everyone in the family knows that Holy Communion really is the Body and Blood of Jesus.)

LET'S PRAY

Lord Jesus Christ, Son of the Living God, You have mercifully provided Yourself to me in the Eucharist. My soul thirsts for You, and You have granted me refreshment. The next time I receive You in Holy Communion, help me pause to appreciate the beauty of Your gift. When I hear or read Scripture passages related to the Eucharist, help me to drink these words in and to penetrate this mystery ever more deeply. I bless You, Lord Jesus. I adore You, and I praise You. Thank You for saving me from sin and death, for quenching my thirst for eternal life. Please bless my family, friends, and all of my loved ones. Forgive my sins and help me remain in a state of grace—refreshed and strengthened by the Eucharist to love and serve You by loving and serving those around me. Amen.

DEEPER CONVERSATION

Read:
- 1 Corinthians 11:23–29
- Questions 274, 277–279, and 188–191 in the *Compendium***

> "The Church accepts and venerates as inspired all 46 books of the Old Testament and the 27 books of the New."
> *Catechism of the Catholic Church, no. 138*

**The Compendium of the Catechism of the Catholic Church (Compendium) is available at www.vatican.va/archive/ccc/index.htm

RESTING ▼ FORGIVING ▼ BEING FREE ▼ AND MORE

NOTES

Use this space to jot down some of your thoughts for discussion.

Discussion 2

Let's Talk About . . .
Where You Live and the Sacrament of Penance

Everyone lives somewhere. And not just in a geographic location, but a physical residence—a house, apartment, etc. You may not think about it much, but where you live requires a certain amount of upkeep. Heaters and, in some cases, air conditioners need to be maintained—that sort of thing. And if serious damage of some sort occurs to your residence, a repair must be made. Maintenance and repair of dwellings, or of bodies—or of souls—is absolutely essential for your life.

 LET'S LISTEN

➤ We all sin. Sin damages and has the potential to destroy your relationship with our loving Father.

➤ Because He loves us God has revealed to us the usual way, the "ordinary means," to make peace. He expects us to celebrate the Sacrament of Penance in order to repair the damage of sin and maintain our ability to do what's right. (See CCC 1497.)

➤ Only a priest can hear a sacramental confession. He has received from God the power to forgive (absolve from) sin.
(See CCC 1495.)

RESTING ▼ FORGIVING ▼ BEING FREE ▼ AND MORE

- How do you celebrate the Sacrament of Penance?
  Three actions are required of you, then one of the priest:
    - You desire to turn away from sin. You *repent*.
    - You personally confess your sins to the priest, who absolves you in Jesus' name.
    - You intend to repair damage caused by your sins.
      (See CCC 1491.)
- The priest gives you a *penance* to do to help repair sin's damage. Sometimes your penance involves prayer; other times it may include additional action aimed at satisfying a wrong done through sin. (See CCC 1494.)
- If your desire to turn away from sin comes from anything other than love of God, it is considered imperfect. Perfect contrition isn't motivated by fear of punishment. Contrition is good. Perfect contrition should always be your goal. (See CCC 1492.)
- The process of looking at your life and sinful behaviors is called examining your conscience. After you do this it is necessary that you confess to a priest any serious sins not previously confessed. (See CCC 1493.)
- Once we've confessed a sin, received absolution, and done penance, our sin is wiped away. It is good to confess even our venial sins so that we can enjoy the full benefits of this sacrament.
- What are the effects of this Sacrament of Penance?
    - Peace with God by which you recover grace.
    - Peace with the Church—who we help by our good actions and harm with our sinful behavior.
    - Forgiveness of deadly or mortal sin which, if unconfessed, could lead to eternal punishment.
    - Relief from at least some of the physical consequences resulting from our sins; this is why our penance is so important.

- o Serenity of conscience, consolation, good old peace of mind!
- o Finally, "...an increase of...strength for the Christian battle" (CCC 1496)

LET'S REFLECT

Living a Christian life, like maintaining a house or apartment, is in some ways a constant battle. Celebrating the Sacrament of Penance at regular intervals—monthly is a challenging yet very beneficial goal—is an excellent practice for preventative maintenance as well as any needed repairs to your spiritual house. Even if deadly sin is absent, the grace you gain through this sacrament helps you avoid falling into minor faults of various sorts. Your entire life will rest peacefully on the solid foundation of God's forgiving love.

> *"We live in times when Confession lines can be short and psychiatrist lines long. Certainly there are cases when psychological guidance and even related medication is much needed. Yet I wonder, if more people celebrated the Sacrament of Penance regularly, would more people be on even footing when our inner life is concerned?"* (See CCC 1486.)

RESTING ▼ FORGIVING ▼ BEING FREE ▼ AND MORE

LET'S TALK!

1. Why does it not hurt self-esteem to state frankly, "We all sin?"

2. What sins come to mind that seem particularly damaging to our relationship with the God Who loves us more than we can imagine? (Regarding any recent sin on your part, don't deny yourself the comfort and other benefits of celebrating the Sacrament of Penance.)

3. If a friend doesn't believe in "going to Confession," how might you point out the difference between possible ways of being forgiven and the ordinary means revealed to us out of love by God?

4. In our Church's eyes, what is the relationship between power and service?

5. We hurt the Body of Christ—our Church—if we behave sinfully. How does this truth relate to the Sacrament of Penance?

6. "A clear conscience makes a soft pillow." What do you think?

7. What is "the Christian battle"?

8. What might be the effects from you celebrating Penance monthly?

ON A RELATED NOTE

Confession stays in the confessional.
➢ Anything you confess to a priest remains in the confessional; this is called the sacramental seal. Priests, and even the civil law, take this sacramental seal very seriously. In the same way that

professional secrets must be kept (for example, doctor-patient confidentiality) and you wouldn't spread harmful information about someone if it was revealed to you confidentially, the seal of the confessional is considered legally and morally unbreakable. (See CCC 2511.)

Refusing God's grace is risky business.
- ➢ God has revealed to us that "[w]hen he comes at the end of time to judge the living and the dead, the glorious Christ will reveal the secret disposition of hearts and will render to each man according to his works and according to his acceptance or refusal of grace" (CCC 682). When we sin, we refuse God's grace. If unrepentant, we risk eternal punishment—the ultimate death!

"I've got some good news, and some . . . good news!"
- ➢ Out of love Jesus freely offered Himself to save us from sin and death. God actually sent His Son, out of love, so that sins may be forgiven. This is truly and literally good news for your life as well as that of your friends, family, and every person. (See CCC 620, 621.)

 ## DRIVING IT HOME

Ask your parents if your family can go to celebrate the Sacrament of Penance together. (Warning: you may want to give them this installment of *Let's Talk* first.)

RESTING ▼ FORGIVING ▼ BEING FREE ▼ AND MORE

LET'S PRAY

At Mass we are absolved from venial sin during the Penitential Rite. Early on, our priest invites us to call to mind our sins. Let us pray together a prayer adapted from this rite:

> I confess to almighty God and to you my brothers and sisters that I have sinned through my own fault—in my thoughts and in my words, in what I've done and what I've failed to do. And I ask the Blessed Mary ever-Virgin, all the angels and saints—and you my brothers and sisters—to pray for me to the Lord our God.
>
> You were sent to heal the contrite, Lord have mercy. You came to call sinners, Christ have mercy. You plead for us at the right hand of the Father, Lord have mercy.
>
> May almighty God have mercy on us, forgive our sins and bring us to life everlasting. Amen.

 DEEPER CONVERSATION

Read:
- Hebrews 4:14–16
- Questions 296–312 in the *Compendium*

NOTES

Use this space to jot down some of your thoughts for discussion.

Let's Talk About . . . Getting some Rest and the Anointing of the Sick

Discussion 3

Hard as it is sometimes, we all need to get a reasonable amount of rest. Without proper rest, odds are we might get sick. Not only does our Church guide us in terms of getting rest, but she also definitely has something to say about handling serious illness—something worth talking about.

 ## LET'S LISTEN

- Special grace is available to Christians suffering from serious illness or dealing with various effects of very advanced age; this grace is available through the Sacrament of the Anointing of the Sick. (See CCC 1527.)

- This sacrament is definitely appropriate when a believer approaches danger of death due to sickness or advanced age. (See CCC 1528.)

- Any time a Christian is seriously ill, the Sacrament of the Anointing of the Sick should be celebrated. If a previous serious illness becomes worse, the sacrament may be celebrated again. (See CCC 1529.)

RESTING ▼ FORGIVING ▼ BEING FREE ▼ AND MORE

- ➢ A priest or bishop administers the sacrament using special oil blessed by the bishop himself. (In exceptional situations, the priest celebrating the sacrament may be the one who blesses the oil.) (See CCC 1530.)
- ➢ How is the Anointing of the Sick celebrated?
  - o The forehead and hands are anointed. (Byzantine or Eastern Catholics may have other parts of their body anointed.)
  - o These anointings are accompanied by the priest's or bishop's prayer asking our loving Father to send this sacrament's special grace. (See CCC 1531.)

LET'S REFLECT

The special graces sent in the Anointing of the Sick help bring these effects: The suffering person unites to Jesus' suffering for her or his good and the good of all His Church. The ill or very old person enjoys strength, peace, and courage so that suffering occurs in a Christ-like way. If celebrating the Sacrament of Penance isn't feasible, the sick one's sins are forgiven. If it will ultimately help to save this person's soul, physical health may be restored. The person is prepared to pass over into everlasting life. (See CCC 1532.)

> *"I don't want to get sick. That would be crazy. Yet I know that if illness comes my way, all is not lost. Even in sickness God's presence and comfort is real for me, my loved ones and all people. In the Anointing of the Sick, as in all seven sacraments, we encounter Jesus Who shares our human suffering and loves us with His Sacred Heart."*

# LET'S TALK!

1. Have you or someone you know ever been seriously ill? Do you know anyone who is very advanced in years? In any of these cases has the Anointing of the Sick been celebrated? If so, please describe the experience.

2. What do you think it means for a suffering person to unite her or his suffering with that of Jesus? How can you see to it that the Anointing of the Sick is used when appropriate by people you know, including yourself?

3. Ask each member of your discussion group what it means to suffer in a Christ-like way. Share among yourselves how each of you feels about the truth that physical health may be restored by the Anointing of the Sick, but only if this healing contributes to the believer's salvation.

ON A RELATED NOTE

Body and soul are related.
> "'Man, though made of body and soul, is a unity' (*GS* 14 § 1). The doctrine of the faith affirms that the spiritual and immortal soul is created immediately by God" (CCC 382). It's no surprise that which affects our body can affect our soul, and vice-versa. "As a result of original sin, human nature is weakened in its powers; subject to ignorance, suffering, and the domination of death; and inclined to sin..." (CCC 418).

RESTING ▼ FORGIVING ▼ BEING FREE ▼ AND MORE

Rest is important.
- ➤ "Every Christian should avoid making unnecessary demands on others that would hinder them from observing the Lord's Day" (CCC 2195). Getting some rest is a part of the Lord's Day, Sunday. We should rest a bit—and allow others to do so.

Death shouldn't come in certain ways.
- ➤ "Intentional euthanasia, whatever its forms or motives, is murder. It is gravely contrary to the dignity of the human person and to the respect due to the living God, his Creator" (CCC 2324). Even suffering can have meaning and value to the eyes of faith. "Suicide is seriously contrary to justice, hope, and charity. It is forbidden by the fifth commandment" (CCC 2325). Intense suffering can lead to suicidal thoughts; we should take initiative against suicide, not just because it's against a commandment, but because life (even when it brings suffering) is always God's preference until He chooses to call us home.

 ## DRIVING IT HOME

Ask a parent or someone older if they've heard of Extreme Unction. Tell them that this sacrament is now known as the Anointing of the Sick and that, rather than waiting for imminent death, our Church now invites us to celebrate the sacrament any time a physical healing or strengthening seems desirable. Inform them that, if you ever become seriously ill, you'd like them to see to it that the Anointing of the Sick is celebrated.

LET'S PRAY

Lord God, heavenly Father, help us to penetrate the mystery of suffering, illness, and death, and, if not to understand it, then to accept these realities as unfathomable parts of your ultimately wise plans.

Jesus, Suffering Servant, you show us that out of suffering and apparent defeat can come some of life's greatest treasures. Help us to retain our hope even when suffering comes so that, rather than despair, we follow your triumphant example.

Holy Spirit, you shower special grace on those celebrating the Anointing of the Sick. Grant us too some share of that grace so that we prudently avoid suffering and, when serious illness is inevitable, we have recourse to your grace through this sacrament. Amen.

DEEPER CONVERSATION

Read:
- James 5:13–15
- Questions 313–320 in the *Compendium*

RESTING ▼ FORGIVING ▼ BEING FREE ▼ AND MORE

NOTES

Use this space to jot down some of your thoughts for discussion.

Let's Talk About . . .
Your Plans and the Sacrament of Holy Orders

Discussion

"Holy Orders." What?! Who's ordering whom around? You think off and on about plans for your future. Part of planning is something called *discernment*—listening to God telling you what will make you happy. (Remember: He has a specific plan for your life.) So let's talk about something specific that will affect your future— maybe personally, maybe indirectly. But always, Holy Orders is worth discussing.

 LET'S LISTEN

- You are part of a priestly people. Your baptism gives you a share in Jesus' priesthood; this participation is called the common priesthood of the faithful. (See CCC 1591.)
- To serve God's people a small but important percentage of men participate in Jesus' priesthood in a unique way. They receive the Sacrament of Holy Orders—they serve in the name and person of Jesus in His Church, the Body of Christ (like your head serves an entirely unique role for your body). (See CCC 1591.)
- A man (in Latin, *vir*) who has received Baptism and whose suitability to serve in Holy Orders has been discerned carefully is

the only person our Church ordains to the ministerial priesthood. As the Body of Christ, the Church has a unique responsibility and right to call men to serve in the Person and name of Jesus—our Body's living Head. (See CCC 1598.)

➤ Priests receive power from God. Priests teach the people (like Jesus the Prophet), conduct holy, sanctifying worship (like Jesus the Priest), and lovingly govern us (like Christ the King). (See CCC 1592.)

➤ Early on, Holy Orders began to consist of three degrees: bishop, priest, and deacon. We could no sooner speak of ourselves as Church without these ordained ministries than a human body can be alive with nothing from the neck up. (See CCC 1593.)

➤ Your bishop has the fullness of Holy Orders. He is a successor to the twelve apostles. Your bishop helps guide the Church's mission with leadership by Saint Peter's successor—the Bishop of Rome—our Pope. (See CCC 1594.)

LET'S REFLECT

Every diocesan priest you know serves as a co-worker united with the bishop. The early word for priest was *presbyter* (elder). Priests form around the bishop a *presbyterium*, a college of priests who help their bishop. (See CCC 1595.) What is a deacon? He is ordained for tasks of service. Though not a priest, he serves a unique role in ministry of the Word, worship, governance, and charity. Like priests, a deacon serves under the loving authority of his bishop. (See CCC 1596.) The laying on of hands (by a bishop) signifies the Sacrament of Holy Orders. A special prayer asks your loving Father to grant the man being ordained the graces needed to serve. (See CCC 1597.) Once ordained, a man is marked forever with a unique sacramental character as deacon, priest, or bishop. (See CCC 1600.)

> *"'Priests are people, too.' Of course they are! Priests struggle in the same ways I do, and experience true happiness in the same gifts God gives all people. Priests, though, have accepted a special gift from God—one that helps them serve His people in unique and important ways. 'God bless all priests as they serve His holy people!'"*

LET'S TALK!

1. What's the difference between the common priesthood of the faithful and ordained, ministerial priesthood?
2. The sixth bullet point above refers to something called the "apostolic succession." Based on the point, what does this term mean?
3. What, if any, role do deacons play in your parish or diocesan church?
4. What are some positive ways that a man who has received Holy Orders has affected your life?
5. What role do you see Holy Orders serving in your future plans, either personally or a bit less directly?

RESTING ▼ FORGIVING ▼ BEING FREE ▼ AND MORE

6. What would you say if one of your male friends says he thinks God may be calling him to priesthood? (Remember the importance of Holy Orders.) What would your other friends say? What are some signs that God may be making that call?

7. Who among your male friends might make a good priest?

ON A RELATED NOTE

Bishops lead their particular Church.
➢ "Helped by priests, their co-workers, and by the deacons, the bishops have the duty of authentically teaching the faith, celebrating divine worship, above all the Eucharist, and guiding their Churches as true pastors..." (CCC 939).

Holy Orders do not add dignity.
➢ "The equality of men concerns their dignity as persons and the rights that flow from it" (CCC 1945). The reservation of ordination to males should never be perceived as a negative statement on women. Because priesthood is a call, it is not a right that every person has. All persons, though, have equal dignity in every way.

DRIVING IT HOME

What would your parents say if a son of theirs (or a male child of a friend) expressed a desire for Holy Orders? You might share with your parents at least some of what you've read in this installment of *Let's Talk*.

YOUR PLANS AND THE SACRAMENT OF HOLY ORDERS

LET'S PRAY

Loving Father, thank you for the gift of Holy Orders. Help us to understand the importance and beauty of this sacrament ever more deeply. Help us see the role that Holy Orders will serve in our life and in the lives of friends and loved ones.

Jesus, as Head of your living Body—our Church—you call men to serve your priestly people in the unique sacrament of Holy Orders. May those you are calling today have the grace to hear and the courage to answer so we may enjoy your presence as Priest, Prophet, and King.

Holy Spirit, you know that Holy Orders requires special graces and comfort. Bless all our priests along with our bishops and deacons so they may continue to serve with love, energy, and wisdom. Amen.

 **DEEPER CONVERSATION**

Read:
- ➤ John 20:21–23
- ➤ Questions 322–336 in the *Compendium*

RESTING ▼ FORGIVING ▼ BEING FREE ▼ AND MORE

NOTES

Use this space to jot down some of your thoughts for discussion.

Let's Talk About . . . Your Strengths and the Sacrament of Marriage

Discussion 5

You have strengths—maybe a couple, maybe several. You may have an outstanding talent. Or, you may be a well-rounded person who is pretty good at several things but not great at any one thing. (By the way, just knowing that about yourself is a strength.) No doubt about it, God has given you gifts, interests, and abilities.

 ## LET'S LISTEN

- ➤ One of the reasons that God gives you certain strengths is to help tell you what He has in mind for your life. For most of us, our loving Father has in mind marriage.
- ➤ Marriage is a gift from God. Marriage is good for the man and woman, helping them have and educate their children. Jesus honors marriage so much that it is one of His Church's seven sacraments. (See CCC 1660.)
- ➤ Real power comes to spouses through this Sacrament of Matrimony: the grace to love each other as Jesus loves our Church. Love is perfected, unity is strengthened, and woman and man are made ever more healthy, happy, and holy.
(See CCC 1661.)

RESTING ▼ FORGIVING ▼ BEING FREE ▼ AND MORE

- The basis of marriage is man and woman consenting to give themselves to each other so to live a covenant of fruitful, faithful love. (See CCC 1662.)
- Because marriage is a public state of life, it makes sense to celebrate it publicly. The priest (or other Church-authorized person), along with the assembly of God's people, has a key place in celebrating this sacrament. (See CCC 1663.)
- What is essential to marriage?
  - unity
  - indissolubility (permanence of unity)
- openness to fertility (see CCC 1664)
- What is incompatible with marriage's unity?
  - polygamy (trying to have more than one spouse)
  - divorce (trying to separate what God has joined sacramentally)
  - refusing fertility (thereby turning marriage from its supreme gift: children) (see CCC 1665)
- The bond of marriage cannot be broken. A decree of nullity—not the same as divorce—can help couples who were not joined sacramentally; this decree may be sought by those obtaining a divorce according to secular law. Without a decree of nullity, a person who tries to remarry (and whose sacramental spouse is still alive) goes against what our loving Father has revealed through Jesus for our own good.
- Someone who "remarries" after a divorce, while not separated from our Church, has taken an action that denies him or her access to the reception of Holy Communion. Educating their children in our Catholic faith is the best way for such people, until remedying their marriage situation, to live as followers and friends of Jesus.

LET'S REFLECT

Why is marriage so important? Among other reasons, marriage sets up a home where children receive their primary education in Catholic faith; because of this "...the family home is rightly called 'the domestic church,' a community of grace and prayer, a school of human virtues and of Christian charity" (CCC 1666). Successful marriage takes certain strengths, strengths animated by the unique grace of this sacrament. Your strengths, although only a part of the whole vocational picture, could be one sign that God may be calling you to marriage. Marriage is indeed a call from God. He calls every person to a specific state of life in our Church. Whether God is calling you to marriage will become clearer as you actively and prayerfully discern your vocation.

> *"God—do you really want me to be married? I know the odds are in favor of this, given Your call to most people for married life. Married life when lived according to Your will is a great blessing. Please guide my friends and me as we continue discerning your call."*

RESTING ▼ FORGIVING ▼ BEING FREE ▼ AND MORE

LET'S TALK!

1. What are your strengths?

2. How might at least some of your strengths be helpful in the state of married life? Ask each member of your discussion group whether they see themselves as eventually getting married? Why or why not? (You might point out that God has already decided if you'll be happiest married or not; the key is to discern what He has in mind for you.)

3. Some would argue that marriage is entirely man-made and that we're free to redefine it if we'd like. Based on what you've read, what is your response?

4. People who remain single after a certain age often get pressured to "find someone and get married." Why would you advise against such pressure?

ON A RELATED NOTE

Here comes the bride.
➤ Our Church is somewhat of a mystery. A mystery in a good sense—as in, just when you think you've got her figured out, you discover something interesting that helps you appreciate her even more. One way of understanding our Church is that she is the Bride of Jesus; He loves her and sacrifices Himself for her.
(See CCC 808.)

Maleness and femaleness are gifts.
- ➤ Male-female imagery only makes sense if we understand and appreciate what it means to be a man, what it means to be a woman. Our maleness or femaleness is a gift from God who gives great dignity to both. All of us should acknowledge and accept our sexual identity. (See CCC 2393.)

Some actions offend marriage.
- ➤ Adultery (a married person and someone other than this person's spouse having sex) is considered a grave offense against the dignity of marriage. Similarly grave offenses are divorce, polygamy, and sex between persons who have not made the marriage covenant with each other. The latter is sometimes referred to as free union. (See CCC 2400.)

DRIVING IT HOME

Tell your parents that the official teaching of the Church is that their home is a domestic church. Tell them also of your understanding that the grace of marriage makes love possible in good times and bad, and that, if God calls you to marriage, you hope to make good use of this grace.

LET'S PRAY

Loving Father, you have given me strengths. I thank You for these gifts. You are calling me to a specific state of life in Your Church. Help me, Lord, to discern Your call. Help me to know that the call is there, to listen for it, to hear it, and to answer it. You speak to me in many ways: in Scripture, in Church teaching, in loved ones, in life events, and in my heart when I am quietly prayerful and let You in. I know that no matter what state of life You call me to, You will make grace available to me, grace to live life in ways that please You and bring about my own greatest joy and happiness. Thank You, God, for Your call. Thank you, Jesus, for Your love. And thank You, Holy Spirit, for the gifts You give to me. Amen.

DEEPER CONVERSATION

Read:
- Mark 10:1–12
- Questions 337–350 in the *Compendium*

NOTES

Use this space to jot down some of your thoughts for discussion.

Let's Talk About . . .
Your Decisions and Freedom

Discussion 6

Decisions. We all make them. Big ones and little ones, day in and day out. Oftentimes people try to persuade you to make one decision or another. So you weigh the pros and cons of different options: the costs and benefits, the pluses and minuses. Persuasion and decisions are parts of your life nearly every day.

 LET'S LISTEN

- ➤ The very fact that you can make a decision reflects a gift that your loving Father has given you—namely, free will. From the very instant you were conceived in your mother's womb, you were oriented toward using freedom to move toward God. (See CCC 1711.)

- ➤ The grace of God enhances your life of following the moral law. Your moral life—using the gift of freedom to make right decisions—is leading you to its highest point: the glory of heaven. (See CCC 1715).

- ➤ Only humans are free in the moral sense; your gift of freedom makes you responsible for decisions you make. (See CCC 1745.)

- It is true that circumstances can sometimes affect your responsibility for a decision (for example, you're less responsible for a decision you make under threat of bodily harm). In most instances, though, a mature person simply takes responsibility for her or his decisions. (See CCC 1746.)
- Freedom is so important that your Church considers it, especially in moral and religious matters, to be an absolute requirement of human dignity. Free will used responsibly, though, keeps you from feeling you have a right to do or say absolutely anything. (See CCC 1747.)
- All of this gets at the question of what makes human decisions right or wrong, good or bad. The morality of human acts consists of three main aspects:
  - the object (What specific action is being considered?);
  - the intention (What is the goal you hope to achieve?); and,
  - the circumstances (What conditions contributed to your act?). (See CCC 1757.)
- For a decision to be morally good
  - the action itself must be appropriate;
  - it must be decided upon with a good goal in mind; and,
  - circumstances must make the decision truly free. (See CCC 1760.) (Notice all three must be present for real morality to guide your use of freedom.)

LET'S REFLECT

An extremely important point: some actions are simply always bad; these are often called *moral absolutes*. Even if my intention or goal is good (for example, I want to provide for my family) I can never freely choose certain objects or actions (murdering my neighbor to get his money to provide for my family) without being responsible for immorality. (See CCC 1761.) Making decisions, then, is very much a part of your life. Your free will is a great gift; it gives you potential to do an immense amount of good and to achieve happiness—even eternal joy. With help from your loving Father, your decisions lead you through life well, until you rest eternally and happily in Him.

> *"Some people say there's no such thing as right or wrong; that whatever I think is right is right for me. In a world with Hitlers this thinking ought to frighten us. I can judge a person's actions without judging that person. Tolerance means loving and respecting all people, not liking and admiring all human behavior."*

 ## LET'S TALK!

1. Explain how, even though you're oriented toward using free will to move toward God, you're still free.

2. How willing are you to take responsibility for your decisions and actions? This is something with which even some adults struggle. If you generally possess the maturity to accept responsibility for how you use God's gift of free will, congratulations! You're ahead of the game!
    o Some people mistakenly perceive your Church as opposing religious and moral freedom; what is your reaction?

3. Distinguish between freedom and license.
4. What makes a decision good?
5. Some would argue that there are no moral absolutes. What is your response?

ON A RELATED NOTE

Lust can affect decisions.
- ➤ The Ninth Commandment concerns desiring to engage in sexual activity that is inappropriate. This commandment warns against lust and motivates us to purify our heart and avoid extremes in various aspects of life. (See CCC 2529, 2530.)

What you strongly desire you are apt to pursue.
- ➤ The Tenth Commandment addresses envy—a sin very serious because it can lead to so many immoral acts. "Envy is sadness at the sight of another's goods and the immoderate desire to have them for oneself…" (CCC 2553). (You can see what kind of actions might be brought about by envy.)
- ➤ How does a baptized person combat envy? Here are some weapons (see CCC 2554):
  - o goodwill
  - o humility
  - o abandonment to the providence of God

In the end it's best not to covet your neighbor's goods anyway. To enter the kingdom of heaven you must be detached from riches. (See CCC 2556.) You know what they say—you can't take it with you!

DRIVING IT HOME

1. The next time a friend tries to persuade you—to talk you into something—tell her or him you have the gift of free will and you're going to use it! (Try not to wag your head back and forth when you say it—your friend will think you have serious attitude problem.) Of course if your friend is trying to talk you into something good, just do it; that's not surrendering free will, it's just being intelligent.

2. Ask your parents the difference between robbing a bank to support a family and working a legitimate job to accomplish the same goal. This is your chance to explain to them that both the object and intention—the goal and the action—must both be good. (Be careful here. If you explain it too well they might use this on you some time.)

LET'S PRAY

Sometimes we use our free will to make immoral decisions. When we do, and our conscience is functioning well, we feel the good kind of guilt—the kind that motivates us to get back on to the right path.

We feel sorrow (contrition) for our sins, and so we may recite this prayer; we make this act of contrition:

O my God I am heartily sorry for having offended you. I detest all my sins because I fear the loss of heaven and the pains of hell, but most of all because they displease you who are all-good and who I should love above all things. I firmly resolve—with the help of your grace—to confess my sins, to do penance, and to amend my life. Amen.

DEEPER CONVERSATION

Read:
- Matthew 24:45–51
- Questions 363–369 in the *Compendium*

> "The four Gospels occupy a central place because Christ Jesus is their center."
> *Catechism of the Catholic Church, no. 139*

NOTES

Use this space to jot down some of your thoughts for discussion.

Let's Talk About . . .
Tobacco and the Fifth Commandment

Discussion 7

Mind over matter? Not always. Most people know intellectually that cigarettes are simply bad for you. Yet many people—even young people who've grown up with the scientific truth about tobacco—are choosing to start smoking. Tobacco-related concerns intersect with an area of our faith that relates directly to human life: the Fifth Commandment, "You shall not kill." Avoiding what harms or destroys human life is definitely something worth talking about.

 LET'S LISTEN

➤ Each human life, from conception until death, is sacred. (See CCC 2319.)

➤ The human person's dignity and our Creator's holiness are very seriously opposed each time a human being is murdered. (See CCC 2320.)

➤ Avoiding murder, though, doesn't mean surrendering your right to take reasonable steps when someone wrongfully or unjustly tries to harm you or those for whom you may be responsible. Defense of self and of the defenseless is not only a right but also—in the case of those responsible for the lives of others or for the common good—a serious duty. (See CCC 2321.)

- Violating the right to be born by aborting an unborn person's life defies the moral law. Our Church considers those participating in abortion knowingly and willingly as placing themselves outside the Christian community. (See CCC 2322.)
- A human embryo is to be cared for, healed, and defended in its integrity just like every human person. (See CCC 2323.)
- When what a person does or fails to do deliberately encourages others toward deadly sin, this is referred to as scandal. (See CCC 2326.)
- War is to be avoided by all reasonable means. (See CCC 2327.)

LET'S REFLECT

Even during armed conflicts, the moral law remains permanently valid. The need to win a war does not justify inhumane treatment of non-combatants, wounded soldiers, and prisoners. (See CCC 2328.) "'The arms race is one of the greatest curses on the human race and the harm it inflicts on the poor is more than can be endured' (*GS* 81 § 3)" (CCC 2329).

"Life and physical health are precious gifts entrusted to us by God" (CCC 2288). Smoking cigarettes (and otherwise using tobacco) is appealing in some ways to many people. Yet human lives can be harmed significantly by excessive smoking in several ways. Habitual use of tobacco may be an indirect, yet significant, transgression of our Fifth Commandment.

> *"God is the author of life. The smartest person in the world can't call life into existence from nothing as God can. Life has become cheap in the eyes of some, and that concerns me. I'll do my best to appreciate God's greatest gift and our most basic human right: life."*

LET'S TALK!

1. Each human person is very good simply by being; that is, we don't have to do or produce anything to have value in God's eyes. What can happen if this truth is misunderstood?

2. What's the difference between harming another person or yourself quickly and dramatically on the one hand, and on the other hand engaging in behavior that over the course of time is likely to cause gradual yet serious harm?

3. Some Christians practice pacifism (nonviolence at all costs) while others reserve the right to use violence if in self-defense or defense of others. Where do you stand?

4. Of all the issues that affect human life, why do you think the right to be born is so vigorously defended by so many Catholics?

5. Human persons who are still embryos aren't always treated with dignity. What are some examples of this? (Hint: abortion is only one of several recent examples.)

6. Why is it seriously sinful to scandalize another person?

7. What do you think it means to avoid war by all reasonable means? What are war crimes? What is the arms race, and why is it decried by our Church?

8. What's the connection between tobacco and the Fifth Commandment?

ON A RELATED NOTE

Baptism gives us life.
➤ "Baptism is the first and chief sacrament of the forgiveness of sins: it unites us to Christ, who died and rose, and gives us the Holy Spirit" (CCC 985).

All three Sacraments of Initiation nurture life.
➤ "Christian initiation is accomplished in three sacraments together: Baptism which is the beginning of new life; Confirmation which is its strengthening; and the Eucharist which nourishes the disciple with Christ's Body and Blood for his transformation in Christ" (CCC 1275). Specifically, "Baptism is birth into new life in Christ. In accordance with the Lord's will, it is necessary for salvation, as is the Church herself, which we enter by Baptism" (CCC 1277).

DRIVING IT HOME

Thank your parents for allowing you to be born (or otherwise welcoming you to the family). Share with them at least some of what you've read in this installment of *Let's Talk*. Invite them to pray, with you, Pope John Paul II's prayer regarding life (following).

LET'S PRAY

O Mary,
bright dawn of the new world,
Mother of the living,
to you do we entrust the *cause of life*.
Look down, O Mother,
upon the vast numbers
of babies not allowed to be born,
of the poor whose lives are made difficult,
of men and women
who are victims of brutal violence,
of the elderly and the sick killed
by indifference or out of misguided mercy.

Grant that all who believe in your Son
may *proclaim the Gospel of life*
with honesty and love
to the people of our time.
Obtain for them the grace
to *accept that Gospel*
as a gift ever new,
the joy of celebrating it with gratitude
throughout their lives
and the courage to *bear witness to it*
resolutely, in order to build,
together with all people of good will,
the civilization of truth and love,
to the praise and glory of God,
the Creator and lover of life. Amen.
(Prayer from Pope John Paul II, *The Gospel of Life*)

RESTING ▼ FORGIVING ▼ BEING FREE ▼ AND MORE

 **DEEPER CONVERSATION**

Read:
- Psalm 139
- Questions 466–486 in the *Compendium*

NOTES

Use this space to jot down some of your thoughts for discussion.

Let's Talk About...
Drugs and Sex

Discussion
8

No kidding. Drugs and sex. These two are often mentioned in the same context; there are probably several reasons for that. Here's a connection between drugs and sex that may not have occurred to you: when sex occurs in its proper context—and there is both a proper and an improper setting for sex—it can give a person the fulfillment that drugs never can. The proper setting for sex and the genuine fulfillment it can bring—now that's something worth talking about.

 LET'S LISTEN

➢ All women and men are called to lead a life of chastity, of which Jesus is the model. (See CCC 2394.)

➢ Your sexuality is to be integrated within yourself; this keeps the beautifully powerful gift of sexuality from dominating you and from being acted upon outside its proper context. Chastity takes practice—especially in the area of self-control. (See CCC 2395.)

➢ Sexual intercourse is to occur between two people of opposite genders who have promised their entire lives to each other

formally and publicly in the Sacrament of Matrimony (marriage). Masturbation, fornication, pornography, and homosexual practices number among the sins contrary to chastity.
(See CCC 2396.)

- ➤ Each of us strives to live chastely depending on what state of life our loving Father has in store for us. Chastity in marriage entails faithful love. Faithful love means, among other things, that the unity of marriage is permanent. (See CCC 2397.)

- ➤ Part of responsible motherhood and fatherhood is taking into account, prayerfully, the number of children in a family as well as their closeness in age (among other considerations). No matter what a couple's goals are here, it would take sex out of its proper context to use anything other than natural methods to help regulate the birth of children. Methods such as direct sterilization and artificial contraception, then, are morally unacceptable.
(See CCC 2399.)

LET'S REFLECT

Many illegal drugs give a feeling of intense pleasure, but one that fades quickly and has several harmful side effects. Sexual intercourse, even outside of its proper setting, can bring pleasure. But the pleasure can soon be overshadowed by the many negative consequences of inappropriate sexual activity. The deepest and most lasting pleasure that sex can bring is when it occurs according to your loving Father's revealed intentions for this powerfully beautiful gift.

DRUGS AND SEX

"Almost every time I get on the internet I see sexuality-related content. Other people are using sexuality to influence me—telling me what to buy, what to listen to, how to dress. Help me, Lord, to be aware of other people's agendas, of how they may try manipulating me, even using Your beautiful gift of sexuality to do so. I'm my own person. And Yours."

LET'S TALK!

1. How are chastity and celibacy related? How do they differ? How might they be said to complement each other?

2. What, if any, illegal drugs are you aware of being used by people? What is it exactly that you think people are after when they use illegal drugs?

3. What are ways that sexuality can dominate a person? Share your thoughts on the statement that chastity includes an apprenticeship in self-mastery.

4. What are some of the negative consequences of sexual activity occurring in ways contrary to the virtue of chastity? What exactly would you say people are after who use the gift of sexuality in inappropriate ways?

5. Anybody got a problem with faithful love?

6. Why is it still true that the unity of marriage is permanent?

7. Describe what you think family life would be like—as well as the impact on society and culture in general—if everyone (or nearly everyone) treated sexuality in the ways your heavenly Father intends for this beautiful, powerful gift.

53

8. What's the connection between tobacco and the Fifth Commandment?

ON A RELATED NOTE

You were made to use all God's gifts properly.
> The human person "...is by nature and vocation a religious being..." (CCC 44). You are called to enjoy your Father's loving gifts—to enjoy them as He intends. It's only natural!

Good habits take some work.
> "The moral virtues grow through education, deliberate acts, and perseverance in struggle. Divine grace purifies and elevates them" (CCC 1839).

If God calls you to parenthood, it's to responsible parenthood.
> "Parents have the first responsibility for the education of their children in the faith, prayer, and all the virtues. They have the duty to provide as far as possible for the physical and spiritual needs of their children" (CCC 2252).

DRIVING IT HOME

> Ask your mom and/or dad what factors influenced their thoughts and feelings about how many children to accept from God and approximately how close in age they might be. As you think about the possibility of God calling you to Holy Matrimony and parenthood (the call to marriage isn't a given, but for most of us it's pretty likely), what role will prayer and other factors play in your decisions about welcoming children into your family

throughout the first decades of married life? (Hint: an old saying tells us that if we wait until we have enough money to have children, we'll never have children!)

➢ Knowing up front that it's intended for use within a marriage, get some reliable information about modern (reliable) fertility awareness principals—often referred to as Natural Family Planning. This information will come in handy if God calls you to marriage and family life. Because new discoveries are made in this field all the time, you might want to share this information with your mom and/or dad.

LET'S PRAY

We thank you, Lord Jesus,
because the gospel of the Father's love,
with which you came to save the world,
has been proclaimed far and wide in America
as a gift of the Holy Spirit
that fills us with gladness.

We thank you for the gift of your Life,
which you have given us by loving us to the end:
your Life makes us children of God,
brothers and sisters to each other.
Increase, O Lord, our faith and our love for you,
present in all the tabernacles of the continent.

Grant us to be faithful witnesses
to your Resurrection
for the younger generation of Americans,

so that, in knowing you, they may follow you
and find in you their peace and joy.
Only then will they know that they
are brothers and sisters
of all God's children scattered
throughout the world.

You who, in becoming man,
chose to belong to a human family,
teach families the virtues which filled with light
the family home of Nazareth.

May families always be united,
as you and the Father are one,
and may they be living witnesses
to love, justice, and solidarity;
make them schools of respect,
forgiveness and mutual help,
so that the world may believe;
help them to be the source of vocations
to the priesthood and the consecrated life,
and all the other forms
of firm Christian commitment.

Protect your Church and the Successor of Peter,
to whom you, Good Shepherd, have entrusted
the task of feeding your flock.
Grant that the Church in America may flourish
and grow richer in the fruits of holiness.

Teach us to love your Mother, Mary,
as you loved her.
Give us strength to proclaim
your word with courage

in the work of the new evangelization,
so that the world may know new hope.
Our Lady of Guadalupe, Mother of America,
pray for us! Amen.

(Prayer of Pope John Paul II for American Families)

 **DEEPER CONVERSATION**

Read:
- Matthew 5:27–28
- Questions 487–502 in the *Compendium*

NOTES

Use this space to jot down some of your thoughts for discussion.

Responses to the Discussion Questions

Discussion 1:
THIRST AND THE EUCHARIST

1. This question is touched upon in another installment. The reaction is usually one of interest because this is often the first time that Mass is described to young people in this way. (When you were a younger, more concrete thinker you may have had trouble grasping this reality; as a high school student more capable of abstract thought you will grow in appreciation of it.)

2. If a worship service other than Mass is attended on these days, it must be in addition to Mass. Missing Mass without a serious reason is a sinful act; those who sin in this way should celebrate the Sacrament of Penance before receiving Holy Communion. (See CCC 2192.)

3. It would be lying through our actions if we pretend to be united with Jesus when we have distanced ourselves from Him with mortal sin. Like a truly good parent, our Church doesn't want us committing acts that will make us feel bad or ashamed because they're wrong. (See CCC 1415.)

4. The closer we are to Christ, the more united we'll be in His Body, the Church. (See CCC 1416.)

5. Although answers may vary, honest, critical thinkers will have to admit some potential benefits.

RESTING ▼ FORGIVING ▼ BEING FREE ▼ AND MORE

Discussion 2:
WHERE YOU LIVE AND THE SACRAMENT OF PENANCE

1. Self-esteem is based on knowing that God made us, God loves us, and God wants us to be happy with Him forever in heaven; it's not based on being sinless. We're all wounded by original sin. We should avoid all personal sin. The fact that God loves us enough to help us avoid sin and to turn back toward Him if we commit sin should boost our self-esteem. (See CCC 1490.)

2. Answers may vary. Don't confess personal sins to each other here, and try celebrating the Sacrament of Penance regularly (for example, monthly).

3. God has clear thoughts on every topic. He makes His thoughts on important matters—like the forgiveness of sins—known to us. Even though in theory God could forgive sins in other ways, His preference is through the Sacrament of Penance. If God's thoughts matter to us, and we want to do His will, then we should seek forgiveness through this sacrament. (See CCC 1497.)

4. Power is for service. Period. Sometimes service can mean correction or even punishment, but power is always to be used in service of others. (See CCC 1495.)

5. The priest reconciles us not only with God but also with our Church—the Body of Christ. (See CCC 1496.)

6. Although answers may vary, it is helpful to point out that of all of life's stresses, a guilty conscience is one we don't need and can avoid with effort and God's grace. (See CCC 1494).

7. Our battle is against sin, evil, and death. We battle sin in our own lives and we fight against its effects in society.

8. Answers may vary. It's crucially important to understand that Penance helps us avoid sin—it's not just for addressing sins already committed. (See CCC 1498.)

YOUR QUESTIONS AND THE ANSWERS THAT GOD PROVIDES

Discussion 3:
GETTING SOME REST AND THE ANOINTING OF THE SICK

1. Answers may vary. We should pursue the celebration of this sacrament whenever it is appropriate to do so.

2. Jesus' suffering has great meaning, as it ultimately leads to our salvation from sin and death. Every suffering person—even in the face of struggles to find meaning or explanation for their suffering—can ask that this suffering be united to that of Jesus. This makes all suffering meaningful and connected, ultimately, to bringing about great goodness. We should contact a priest to anoint the sick when appropriate and needed. We can also attend and encourage others to attend public celebrations of this sacrament. (See CCC 1532.)

3. Although answers may vary, Christ-like suffering includes a peacefulness, a minimization of anger, and a confidence that in the long run all will be well. (Again, see CCC 1532.)

Discussion 4:
YOUR PLANS AND THE SACRAMENT OF HOLY ORDERS

1. Whereas everyone who's baptized has some share in Jesus' priestly, prophetic, and kingly work, only men who are ordained to the ministerial priesthood can represent Christ in uniquely sacramental ways such as consecrating the Eucharist and absolving sins in the Sacrament of Penance. (See CCC 1591 and 1592.)

2. This refers to the unbroken line of succession between the apostles and all Catholic bishops today. (See CCC 1594.)

RESTING ▼ FORGIVING ▼ BEING FREE ▼ AND MORE

3. Answers may vary depending on the local prominence of the permanent deaconate.

4. Although answers may vary, an example would be making the sacraments available.

5. One way or another, priesthood will have an impact on everyone's life. A few may be ordained. Many will be married in front of a priest, and they will likely see their babies baptized by priests. A few may see their sons grow up to be ordained. These are only a few examples.

6. An important sign is several other people suggesting that a young man would be a good priest.

7. Answers may vary. It's good to point out that many of the same traits that make men good husbands and dads can also help them be effective priests. This truth challenges statements like "So-and-so must not be called to priesthood because he'd be a great family man," while of course upholding priestly celibacy. Everyone knows someone who might make a good priest.

Discussion 5:
YOUR STRENGTHS AND THE SACRAMENT OF MARRIAGE

1. Answers may vary.

2. Again, answers may vary.

3. Note that one can get married or refrain from marriage for appropriate or inappropriate reasons. The key is discernment of God's will.

4. A good response based on the reading includes the fact that the marriage covenant is a gift from God Who has revealed marriage's own special laws, which means that we're not free to redefine marriage. (See CCC 1602 and 1603.)

5. God doesn't call everyone to marriage. A person who is well into young adulthood and isn't married may have a vocation other than Matrimony.

Discussion 6:
YOUR DECISIONS AND FREEDOM

1. At any time we can use our free will to move away from God. We are truly free. (See CCC 1711.)

2. Answers may vary.

3. The Church vigorously defends religious liberty. She also upholds the authority of an informed conscience. If she is misunderstood regarding freedom, it's because she doesn't equate liberty with license (doing whatever one wants regardless of the consequences). Freedom is understood as being free to choose the good and true—thus living up to our full human potential. Rights make sense only when responsibility accompanies their exercise. (See CCC 1747.)

4. See answer immediately above.

5. A decision is good when it discerns good methods to pursue good goals; both must be good. (See CCC 1760.)

6. Answers may vary, but the perception of absolutes is basic to human cognition. Even a person arguing that there are no moral absolutes is asserting an absolute. So while in the realm of pure theory it may be interesting to consider an absence of absolutes, the school of daily human activity teaches us otherwise. (See CCC 1761.)

RESTING ▼ FORGIVING ▼ BEING FREE ▼ AND MORE

Discussion 7:
TOBACCO AND THE FIFTH COMMANDMENT

1. On the one hand, people who aren't productive in some way could be seen as unimportant or even, in the extreme, as non-persons (for example, a person who has suffered severe brain damage). It's possible on the other hand to feel no obligation to be productive, which could be squandering gifts and talents given by God for the building of His kingdom. (See CCC 2319.)

2. In the first case there is little opportunity to stop the course of action once it has started; in the latter there are many chances along the way to halt and maybe even undo the damage.

3. Answers may vary. The Church clearly upholds the right to self-defense. (See CCC 2321.)

4. If a person isn't allowed to be born in the first place, then all other rights become irrelevant. (See CCC 2322.)

5. One example would be several human eggs being fertilized in vitro but only one or two of them being implanted while the others are thrown away or frozen in a state of suspended animation.

6. It is seriously sinful to scandalize another because the person who scandalizes risks becoming an indirect cause of evil; this is literally devilish or satanic. (See CCC 2326.)

7. Much negotiation must be attempted before war is even considered. War crimes are behaviors that go beyond what is legitimate action for defense of self and others. The arms race sees countries trying to outdo each other in accumulating powerful weapons—often using resources that are needed elsewhere (for example, education, ethical research, etc.). (See CCC 2327–2329.)

8. Tobacco—especially when abused—can destroy human life.

Discussion 8:
DRUGS AND SEX

1. Chastity and celibacy relate in that, for unmarried persons, they both mean refraining from sexual activity. They're different because, while the celibate state does not change, a person's way of living out chastity changes in an important way when she or he marries; the relationship is now open to chaste sexual intercourse. Celibacy and chastity complement each other in that in various ways celibates help others to live chastely, while married couples can instill in their children an appreciation of celibacy for the sake of God's kingdom, such that children will be open to this call if that is God's will for them. (See CCC 2394.)

2. Answers may vary. People who start using illegal drugs usually do so for social, mind-altering, and/or thrill-seeking reasons. When addiction sets in, they use drugs mainly to feed the addiction.

3. Although answers may vary, one point to bring out is that chastity usually takes effort and focus. (See CCC 2395.)

4. Answers may vary, but remember that the negative consequences aren't just physical. Sin is a result; this is serious business. (See CCC 2396.)

5. While answers may vary, "faithful love" is a concept worth understanding and affirming.

6. God invented marriage. One of the traits He gives it is its lifelong nature. (See CCC 2397.)

7. Our culture gives mixed messages about marriage and sexuality. At some level we can't help but be influenced by what we see and hear, especially through the media. Since God created us and since our sexuality is an important component of our makeup,

it is valuable to understand the Creator's plan and embrace it. Knowing the truth and living it is both freeing and life-giving.